DUTY BOUND

A Conscript's Tale

William B Burkey

Costa Press

PREFACE

National Service was an extension of the WWII conscription, and lasted from 1946 to 1963. Nearly 2,000,000 young men, aged from 18 – 21 served, mainly in the army. It was created to meet the shortage of military manpower required to meet the ever growing commitments in Asia, Africa, Germany and Austria, together with the requirement to support France, Holland, Japan and Korea. Not everyone was required to serve, for example Northern Irish, Gipsies and the racing community. Liverpool Irish and the Glasgow gang members were not required, due to the social problems of the time. However, many people were of the opinion that the discipline of military life would be good for football hooligans and other anti-social groups who were causing unrest.

This is the story of the two years of my life given over to National Service, which many people were of the opinion that it was a waste of time. I disagree. In my case I learned a great deal, both physical and mental. National Service provided me with the opportunity to experience many physical activities that I would not have done if I had not done my time. For instance, I obtained my driving licence before I owned a car and I travelled all over Germany, growing in self-confidence and meeting many interesting people. I also gained several qualifications, including 3 trade test badges and a Royal Army Education Corps Instructor's Certificate, which led me eventually into a new career in teaching and education.

I have not described each individual day, as this would be an impossible task and very boring for the reader. So I have taken as many instances of army life that I can remember some sixty odd years after the events, which I believe will hold the interest of the reader. Obviously the areas of Germany that I describe have changed over the years, but my recollections are of the time 1954 -56.

My thanks to my wife Jo for all her support and for putting up with all the hours I spent typing. To my daughter Wendy, for her encouragement and editing skills and to my son in law Eddie for designing the cover for the book. I used the internet for various stock photographs of vehicles.

Finally, thank you to all the very kind people who bought and read the book and offered their opinions.

William B Burkey Spain 2017.

Call Up

It was Friday evening 22nd January 1954 when I met my mother after work at Brindles Jewellers in Cleveland Street, Chorley, where I was to choose a signet ring as my 21st birthday present from mum and dad.

As we waited for the bus home, mum said, "There was a letter for you this morning," as she delved into her handbag for it.

As I examined the envelope I saw that it had OHMS (On His Majesty's Service) on the right hand top corner, which filled me with dread. It was clearly official. What could it be, I wondered? There was only one way to find out - open it. This I did with trembling fingers, to find that it was my calling-up papers.

REME cap badge REME tie

I was to report to No 1 Training Battalion REME, at Blandford Camp, Dorset on 4th February 1954. What a 21st birthday present that was, particularly as my birthday party was to be held in the Royal Oak Hotel the following evening, attended by my extended family including my fiancé, Jo, who readers met in my book Boyhood Blitz. It had been over three years since I was called for my army medical, so I had really forgotten about the prospect of being called-up.

Jo was naturally not very pleased, as we had become engaged on her 21st birthday in May and we were starting to plan our wedding. However, the thought that I should not go to Blandford did not enter my head, one had to go and make the best of it, which I did. To my surprise I enjoyed the experience. If I had decided not to go, then the police would have issued an arrest warrant for me and I could have been classified as a deserter, which in those days was a criminal offence, with all the ramifications that would ensue.

My national service had been deferred until my 21st birthday because I served an engineering apprenticeship as a machine tool fitter, which included 22 months working in the New Development & Process Drawing Office at English Electric Company in Preston. At the end of this I had been awarded my Ordinary National Certificate in Mechanical Engineering.

My employer was required by law to provide me with a similar job upon my release in two years' time. In my case I returned to the same drawing office and actually to the same drawing board that I had left..

Blandford Camp, Dorset

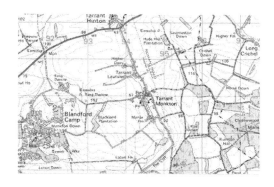

The camp's military history goes back to the 19th century when it was utilised by the Royal Navy as a shutter telegraph station. In November 1914 the Royal Naval Division (RND) established a base depot and training camp on the site, but later moved out in 1918. The Royal Navy were replaced by the Royal Air Force record office, equipment and personnel and discharge centre, until 1919 when the camp was closed down.

In 1939, the camp was reactivated as a mobilization and training centre for reservist called up to meet the threat from Hitler's Germany. Later anti-aircraft units of Royal Artillery trained on the site and it became a battle training camp. From 1946 until 1962 Blandford Camp was used to train national servicemen by the Royal Artillery, The Royal Army Service Corp, REME and the Catering Corps.

This posting was of great interest to both me and my dad, who had been a regular soldier from 1920 to 1930, serving with the Royal Armoured Corps. Being on the army reserve when World War Two broke out, he spent most of the war based at Bovingdon Camp near Blandford, as a tank driving instructor with the Royal Tank Regiment. At the end of the war he was their Chief Driving Instructor. As far as Jo and my mother were concerned, they were not very happy at my departure, but at least they knew where I was going.

Being a good citizen, complete with the small suitcase allowed and a packet of sandwiches, on the 4th of February 1954 I duly caught the train to Manchester Victoria from Chorley. Walking across to Manchester Piccadilly station, I caught the Pines Express to Blandford Forum in Dorset, a journey through the Midlands and South West England, arriving at 5.00pm. By this time the train was full of young men all going to start their National Service. There must have been at least 150 on our train, all between 18 and 21 years of age. Many more travelled from different parts of the country, making up a total of 250 trainees in the intake.

As we all left the train, in the dark of the night, slipping and sliding on the frozen platform, a loud bellowing voice instructed us to climb into a fleet of army lorries waiting in the station yard. We then undertook a thirty-minute journey along snowy and icy roads to Blandford camp. I was the last one in my lorry and so was sat at the tail board, frozen stiff and mesmerised by the view of the icy road along which we were travelling.

Arriving at the camp we were shown into a large room with a long table at one end, where we were allowed to help ourselves to some food and a cup of tea. As I was the first to enter the room I was the first for the food, and as I was looking to find somewhere to sit a voice shouted, "Here you are son, sit here," and like an idiot I did.

Immediately a cloth was whipped around my neck, fortunately covering my food, and I was given the shortest back and sides haircut of my life. This really upset me, as the day before I had been given a haircut by my local barber, who being ex-army had assured me it would pass muster. Just wait till I get back home, I thought. I'll have his guts for garters.

Having been fed and haired, we were then taken to the clothing store where we were issued with our kit. This consisted of virtually two of everything; battle dress uniforms, denim uniforms, shirts, underwear, socks, boots, PE kit, great coat, knife, fork, spoon, tie, cleaning kit and a housewife (the sewing kit). Finally, we were given bedding; sheets blankets and pillow cases. We then had to carry this lot to our barrack room, which was one section of an American Spider - a central spine with three barrack rooms on each side, accommodating 24 beds in each. This was the standard design used by the Americans when they built army camps all over Southern England in preparation for the D-day landings. The building, originally an American WWII army hospital, was in good condition, well heated, with good showers and lots of hot water.

We were instructed by our squad corporal, who was dressed in an immaculate uniform, on how make up a bed block, lay our kit out for inspection and then given details of what we would do the following day. By this time, it was 10 o'clock at night and we had to sew all the buttons onto a set of denim uniform before we could get into bed.

Suddenly the door of the room burst open and a young man staggered in, trailing a large suit case. The corporal demanded to know who he was and where had he been.

"I have walked six miles from the station," he replied in a very broad Northern accent, "and my feet are killing me."

He sat down on a bed and took off his socks and shoes, to show the largest set of bunions I had ever seen. Glowing red they were. The joints of each toe were swollen and stiff, which must have been very painful.

He was then asked, "Which idiot has passed you fit for entry to the army?"

He disappeared the following morning and was discharged two days later.

That ended my first day of national service. There were only 729 days to demob, or as was said, "Roll on death, demob is too far away!" And so to bed.

We were awakened the following morning at 6.00am by our mentor from the previous evening, our squad corporal who had turned into a screaming animal, banging on the beds and lockers with his pace stick. After washing, shaving and dressing, we fell in and marched to breakfast, our first indoctrination into army food. The only thing that I can remember was rinsing our mug, plate, knife and fork, in a large tank of soapy boiling water followed by a further rinse in clear water. Talk about scolding your fingers – ouch!

After breakfast we tided the barrack room and laid our kit out on the bed and fell-in for inspection by the squad corporal. That was when many an untidy bed block was sent flying onto the floor. We soon learnt how to do it properly.

Then followed instructions on how to Blanco our webbing belts and gaiters, polish the brass buckles, and bull the toe and heel caps on our boots. This involved removing the pimples in the leather by using a hot iron or by heating the end of a tooth brush in a candle flame, followed by the application of black shoe polish which was polished using a yellow duster moistened with saliva and moved in small circles. Hence, the term spit and polish. This lead to the question, how many magic circles were there in a tin of Cherry Blossom Shoe Polish?

We were then marched to a large room where we had to complete our Qualifications & Record card (Q&R). This contained all our personal details, qualifications, religion etc. My ever lasting memory of the event was when the lad in front of me was asked his religion.

He said, "Agnostic."

The corporal completing the card replied, "I can't spell that; you are C of E!"

This was followed by our introduction to foot drill, taken by the squad corporal. This was easy for me having been in the Church Lad's Brigade for some eight years, achieving the rank of Warrant Officer Class 2. Being the Battalion Drum Major in the drum and bugle band, my knowledge of basic foot drill was excellent, which gave me great confidence in my initial training.

Church Lad's Brigade

In the afternoon we were taken to the education centre, where we sat a series of tests, including trade tests. This resulted in me being graded Mechanical Draughtsman Grade 3, which was my Corps primary trade.

The next morning, we were marched to the main parade ground to watch the passing out parade of No 3 training battalion, being the intake before ours. This was an eye opener, particularly the very poor quality of the drum and bugle band. A couple of days later I was required to report to the OC's office, for why I did not know. I was marched into his office, were I was quizzed about my time in the CLB. This culminated in the offer to be the drum major of the drum and bugle band. This was of great interest, until it was explained that I would have to sign on as a regular soldier on a minimum of a three-year contract. After all of 3 second's consideration, I respectfully declined the offer, as I did not wish to make the army my career and was sent back to my squad.

The next item of interest was our visit to the stores, wearing our best khaki uniforms and great coats, which were checked by the tailor for fit and appearance. Any alterations were chalked and noted and the altered uniforms were ready some days later.

We then had our first Padres Hour. We were marched to the camp cinema, where we met for the first time the camp Company Sergeant Major (CSM). What a fine figure of a man he was, immaculately turned out in full battle dress and with a voice that could be heard in the next town. He stood on the stage and explained that we were to meet with the padres of the different religions. The order was C of E in the front seats, RC at the back, Non-Conformist in the middle. The order to move was given. When everyone had moved, there was one lad left all on his own. The CSM then marched down the aisle to him and in a loud voice asked him what religion he was.

"Please sir, I am an Agnostic," replied the boy.

"So am I," replied the CSM. "Come with me."

We didn't see the lad for 24 hours.

When he turned up, we asked him where he had been.

"In the cook house peeling potatoes," he replied.

A very quick religious conversion was on the cards, we thought.

By this time, we were settling down to army life of drill, PE, cleaning kit, barracks and inspections. Then came our first medical. What a farce. We had to stand in the nude in front of the medical officer who looked at us with a bored eye, placed his hand under our testicles and told us to cough. That was it. We were all declared A1.

The manner in which we were spoken to, the names we were called, would in today's army be called bullying, in no uncertain terms. But back then we just laughed it off later in the barracks. We had a platoon corporal who was an expert at calling us names. The two best ones he called me were, "I was standing like a pregnant fairy with festered tits," and that, "He would push his pace stick so far up my rectum that it would come down my nostrils and knock my bloody spectacles off." This in spite of the fact that I was one of the best recruits in the platoon.

The most stupid command was when we had a break and ordered to fall out for a smoke, and those who did not smoke had to go through the actions. As a non-smoker along with others, we had to stand there and pretend we were smoking.

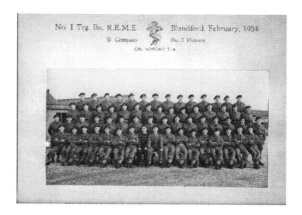

The best parade was, of course, pay parade. This was on Thursday afternoons. We were all lined up in alphabetical order. When your name was called, you marched up to the table, saluted the officer, gave him your surname, the last three numbers of your army number and showed him your Army Pay Book, which was in effect your identity card. You then took a side step to the left and a soldier gave you your pay in cash. This needs some explanation. My army number was 22992585. My pay was £3 per week. I had arranged for my mother to receive the sum of £1. 10 shillings, who had agreed to save it for me, leaving me with the same sum for my weekly spending money. This was quite adequate as I didn't smoke, and we were in a dry camp

Barton Stacy Camp, Hampshire

After two weeks in Blandford, on the 18th February, our draft was split into two parts; one remaining at Blandford and the other moving to Baton Stacey in Hampshire. I was in that group, travelling again by army lorry.

What a sight that camp was. Old wooden barrack blocks, heated by a pot stove fired by coal, to heat a room some 30 feet long by 18 feet wide. The stove was only lit after working hours, with the beds closest to it being the most sought after. A good stoker could have the stove glowing red by bedtime, so at least we went to bed warm. The toilets and showers were very old with a minimum of hot water. This fact alone got you out of bed in the morning, otherwise you were shaving in cold water in the middle of winter.

Hand grenade, Lee-Enfield Rifle, Bren Mk 2, Sten Mk 3

Barton Stacey was where we settled down to serious soldering. Here we were issued with rifles and introduced to the mysteries of rifle drill, as well as the more specialist foot drill. We learnt to throw hand grenades, dummy ones thank goodness, and to shoot on the firing range using our rifles, Sten guns and Bren guns. We also had to learn how to strip the weapons down, clean, lubricate and reassemble them.

After using the weapons on the firing range we then had to learn how to clean them properly. This included pouring boiling water down the barrel to remove the carbon deposits produced by firing the gun. This was repeated until the water ran clean with no deposits in it.

Using a length of cord with a loop on the end, together with a piece of cloth 4" long x 2" wide, called a 'pull through' fastened in the loop, it was pulled through the barrel and repeated until the barrel was dry and shining. The rest of the weapon was then cleaned and oiled, with the woodwork, if any, polished to a high shine.

The examination of the weapons for cleanliness was done on muster parade in the morning. The order was given, 'inspection port arms', which meant having your rifle at 45 degrees across your body. The bolt was then removed and the thumb placed in the breach with the thumb nail facing the barrel. The examiner then looked down the barrel from the front sight and using the light reflected from the thumb nail could see if the inside of the barrel was clean and shining.

During rifle drill, two pennies were placed in the empty magazine, thus producing a good sound when the butte of the rifle was slapped with the hand. It was one more attempt to try and make us as good as, if not better than, the brigade of guard regiments.

One afternoon we were practicing the procedure for what happened when the gun jammed or the magazine was empty when using the Bren gun. The command was, 'mag off, mag on'. One young man was having problems with the exercise and the platoon sergeant gathered us around and started dropping empty mags on the boy's head. This didn't hurt him as he was wearing his tin hat. The sergeant was telling a story as he was doing this. He said that in Malaya in the military cemetery, there was a plot of ground six-foot-long and three-foot-wide and lying in it was his best friend, who was awful with a Bren gun. The look on the young man's face was a picture clearly wishing he was better at the procedure than he was.

One morning on muster parade the sergeant was inspecting the platoon, when he suggested in a loud voice that one young lad had not been washing his neck very well. The next day the same conversation took place, with the addition of an order for me and another lad to take him to the showers and scrub him clean. This we did and that lad never missed an evening shower for the rest of his time at Barton Stacy.

Our period of training was coming to an end and I was very pleased to be selected as the best recruit in our platoon. We then spent many hours practicing for our passing out parade, which included the presentation of certificates. After that the postings were displayed on the barrack notice board in, 'Part 1 orders' and I found that I was to go to Germany. This was great news because it meant that I was entitled to 14 days' embarkation leave before I departed.

However, on the Friday afternoon before we left Barton Stacey, we all had to have our overseas inoculations, or jabs as they were called. This meant a trip to the medical centre, where we were lined up with our shirt sleeves rolled up and passed down two lines of medical orderlies who administered a jab each. That was a total of four in each arm. After tea our task was to clean up the barrack room and get our kit ready for the CO's Saturday morning inspection. Bit by bit people started going down with what was called jab fever, complete with a high temperature, headaches and nausea. The only cure for it was to hop into bed. By 9.00pm or soon after, we were all in the same boat and in bed.

The following morning very early, the platoon sergeant appeared to find people staggering around, with two or three still in bed and unable get up. He immediately set to and made their beds army style and supervised the kit layouts. When the CO appeared he enquired what had been the problem and accepted the reasons and complemented us on a good turnout. He then turned to the corporal who supervised the billet, asking him where he was last evening when this problem had arisen.

The corporal replied, "In the NAFFI, sir."

At which point the sergeant was ordered to place the corporal on a charge.

As a result of our efforts, we were allowed to leave camp and spend the evening in the town of Barton Stacy, which was the first time we had been outside camp for six weeks.

We all thought that our platoon sergeant had been the best on the camp and we had a whip round for him, which in this case was a couple of pint bottles of beer. Two of us were selected to take our gift to him in the sergeant's mess, where he promptly called to his friend for glasses and he shared the beer around. Whilst we were with him I asked about the story of his friend and the Bren gun. It transpired that he was originally in the Leicester Regiment, a very good infantry regiment, serving in Malaya against the communist terrorists, when his best friend lost his life because his gun jammed and he was slow in freeing it and was killed by an insurgent. He then explained that he had transferred to REME, as a drill instructor, in order to gain his substantive rank of sergeant. A good decision as far as we were concerned.

On the Monday we went home on our embarkation leave, complete with all our kit in a large kit bag and wearing greatcoat and full webbing. My train journey took me back to Chorley via London, arriving home in Birch Road at about 5.00pm. After a meal I set off hot footed to go to Jo's house in Lawson Street. When I walked in she jumped up and threw her arms around me. At which point I yelped with pain as she had squeezed on the site of the jabs which were still very tender, red and swollen. Still the welcome was very worthwhile, and I settled down to two weeks' leave.

REME Depot Arborfield Berks

At the end of my leave was another rail journey, this time from Preston to London Euston, then a change to Waterloo and a train to Wokingham in Berkshire. This was the town Jo and I and our two daughters came to live in 1966 when I obtained a lecturing post at Slough College. An army lorry took us to the camp at Arborfield, some six miles away. There I met several friends from Blandford and Barton Stacy, and we caught up with all the news. It appeared that the platoon corporal in Blandford had had a complete breakdown and became the post corporal. The billet corporal at Barton Stacey was reduced in rank for dereliction of duty.

At Arborfield I also met the young man whom we had to supervise having a shower. When he saw me, he picked up his towel and went for a shower. On his return he thanked me for the way he had been treated and explained that he lived in a London tenement with no bathroom and only one cold water tap per landing. I heard later that he had signed on as a regular soldier, to give him a better life than he had at home. So some good did come from National Service for one individual.

The platoon sergeant at Arborfield was an old soldier in many ways. He was waiting for the end of his service and was in charge of the Germany Draft. He had a very lucrative side line selling cigarettes, stockings, ladies' underwear, condoms etc., to the recruits.

The only exciting event which took place there was on one rainy morning when the weather prevented the normal training programme. So the problem of what to do with us that morning after NAFFI break was solved by showing us the Pox Film, as it was known. We all assembled in the cinema to be shown a film on venereal disease. This was horrible, showing infected people with Gonorrhoea and Syphilis together with the effects on wives and families. The worst bit was the showing of an infected penis, complete with sores and other details, which was received with groans and shouts of disbelief. The film was followed by our lunch, at which burnt sausages were served, with the burnt meat protruding from the ends. The squeamish ones left theirs, whilst the brave ones, me included, ate the lot and several more, as many lads couldn't face them, with several going green in the face.

The time came for our departure to Germany. I was promoted to temporary draft corporal for the duration of the journey, with the responsibility of making sure that everybody was where they were supposed to be. Some hope, as I shall recount later. We caught the train at Wokingham Station to Waterloo, complete with all our kit. There we loaded our kit onto an army lorry and we then had to take the tube from Waterloo to Liverpool Street Station. Can you imagine the sight of over twenty squaddies in single file going up and down the escalators and changing platforms? I was very pleased that I got my lot safely there, until one lad informed me that he was going home to see his girlfriend, as she only lived two stations down the line. Did I panic! But fortunately he came back in time to catch the train to Harwich for the boat to the Hook of Holland.

The boats, or ships, that the army used on this route, were converted tank landing craft left over from the war, and being flat bottomed and in a rough sea, boy did it roll. There was a lot of seasickness about but fortunately I was not affected. The boat decks were the converted tank holds, which had bunks installed three high, with very little room for your kit. We arrived at the Hook of Holland after an overnight journey, in time for breakfast, which was taken in the NAFFI.

I saw a queue of people lining up at a kiosk and asked someone what they were queuing for.

"Cigarettes," he replied.

"What?" I said, "At 3s,6p for twenty?"

"No," came the reply. "One shilling for twenty."

I joined the queue pretty quickly. Hang on, I hear you say. You told us that you didn't smoke. But what I didn't say was that I stopped smoking when I was eighteen years old, because I couldn't afford it. At those prices I could, and I didn't stop for another ten years until I had my tonsils out.

Duisburg Germany

After a smoky journey we finally arrived at Duisburg at 4 Inf. Workshops REME, where we were held on draft until we were posted to a permanent unit. The only notable event which took place there, was an evening visit to the camp beer bar for a night out. Within our group was a lad called Arthur, who had served his apprenticeship at Guinness's Brewery in Park Royal, London. There, once employees turned 18 years of age, they were allowed one pint of Guinness per day at the end of their shift. Arthur, therefore, considered himself a hardened drinker and thought that the German beer would not have any effect on him. After a couple of pints, we decided that bed was calling and left the beer bar through the main door, which was at the top of 10 steps. As the cold air hit Arthur, the beer took effect and he fell from the top to the bottom of the steps, without hitting a single one. We picked him up and took him to bed - the hardened drinker. He never did live that night down.

Whilst we were in Duisburg, three of us went for a walk through the neighbourhood housing estate.

A couple of German youngsters riding past on their bicycles, shouted, "English bastards fuck off!"

It was suggested to us by a soldier passing-by that we should ignore them, as they didn't know any better. That was the only time that I ever encountered that type of abuse during my time in Germany. Indeed, it was always the opposite, as we were received with kindness and good behaviour wherever we went.

Dortmund Germany

After two weeks, we were posted to 6 Infantry Workshops REME, which was located on what is now named Westfalendamm, or Route 1, in Dortmund. The barracks were ex-German military and very well appointed and named Redesdale Barracks. The sleeping accommodation was in rooms containing two, four, or six beds, with ample toilets and showers, with lots of hot water. The cook house as it was called, or dining room, was on the ground floor, with the NAFFI on the same floor, but at the further end of the building with a separate entrance. The Warrant Officers' and Sergeants' Mess were in the building opposite, again on the ground floor, with the unit stores on the end. The offices and education centre were on the first and second floors. The workshops were located further inside the unit, grouped around the parade ground. They consisted of Motor Mechanics, Fitters, Welders, Electronics, Recovery Section and the Stores Department. There were approximately 150 personnel located in the unit. This was the posting that ensured that a regular delivery of mail became the norm. On most days I received a letter from Jo and I wrote her a reply. It was this exercise that kept us in touch with each other and kept the flame of our love alive.

The dreaded day arrived when my name appeared on orders for guard duty. This required falling in on the parade ground at 17.00 hours in full best kit. Boots bulled like glass, brasses shining like the sun, webbing blancoed and immaculate and uniform pressed to razor creases. The guard fell-in and were inspected by the orderly officer of the day. One of the six members of the guard, i.e. the best turned out, was designated Stick Man. This meant that you did not do any patrol duties, but made the tea during the night and could sleep in the guard room when not required. To my surprise, I was Stick Man on my first guard duty. I also won the award on the next two guard duties that I was on. This obviously did not go down well with the other lads and to solve the problem I was changed to the duty clerk rota. This meant that I had to sleep in the orderly room and answer the telephone etc., during the night. This was a cushy number most nights.

One night, the telephone rang about 2.00am. Without any preamble, the voice on the other end stated, "Immediate compassionate message operate Pip Emma."

The message was for one of the lads whose mother had been taken seriously ill in the UK and he was to travel home immediately. Full instructions for travel were given. I had to repeat the message back, to ensure that I had received it correctly. I then had to call the Orderly Sergeant and Orderly Officer. The lad was awakened, packed some kit, the orderly driver was summoned and he was on his way, 30 minutes after the receipt of the message. I had not received any training in this exercise, and didn't want to have to do it again.

Because my trade was draughtsman, for my daytime post I was attached to the education centre and assisted the Royal Army Education Corps staff sergeant with the library and also helped with the number of soldiers who had difficulty in reading and writing, particularly with writing letters home. I also helped in the Orderly Room, which was the Chief Clerk's country. He was a tarter, but very good at his job. It was here that I met the lad who became my best pal, Johnny.

Driving

Austin 3 ton lorry

My next adventure was learning to drive in an Austin 3-ton lorry, with the engine in the cab, the gearbox handle behind the engine and located somewhere behind your left shoulder. If you stalled the engine, which I did frequently at the start, the engine would run backward for a few revs and a cloud of exhaust fumes would enter the cab, via the air filter, causing driver and instructor to bail out!

Our driver training took place on an abandoned air field where we could practice all the required skills and manoeuvres, without causing any damage. This flughafen later became the site for Dortmund Airport. I trained there for three weeks before being let out on the roads in traffic. The only problem that I had was coping with the trams in the centre of Dortmund.

On one cross country exercise, having entered a level crossing, the gate in front of me closed as did the rear one. I had to sit there in between the two sets of lines as two high speed trains passed through the crossing, one in front and one behind me. Believe me I was shaking like a leaf when the gates opened and I could drive on. My instructor was highly amused and then explained that what had just happened was standard practice. I was relieved to know I wasn't the only one to have experienced that.

I then had to take my test. The examiner was the Staff Sergeant in charge of the motor mechanics platoon. We first of all did the vehicle check; oil, water, tyres, lights etc. Then off we went, around a course of cross country and built up areas. I then had to map read for the tester, while he drove to a given location.

When we returned to the unit, I had to pull up in front of the accommodation block and reverse along the block, around to the back, just using the wing mirrors. This was going well until we came behind the block when the lorry started to lift up at the back with the wheels spinning. The tester jumped out and hit the roof.

Whilst we had been out somebody had dumped a lorry load of coke and not shovelled it into the coke hole. Fortunately for me he saw the funny side of it and so I passed my driving test.

Austin 1 ton lorry

Because I was now a certified army driver I was given charge of an army vehicle, which meant that as the nominated driver I was responsible for the daily maintenance of the vehicle and was the driver when the vehicle was in use. On one occasion, having taken a party of soldiers to an exhibition, I was driving back to Dortmund. Passing down a narrow village road I met a farmer on his tractor towing four trailers, which they did frequently. As I tried to overtake him, he deliberately flicked his steering wheel, which caused the trailers to snake and hit the front wing of the lorry, causing a large dent. Fortunately, I had an officer in the cab with me, who verified the details when I filled in the accident report form. That was my first and only traffic accident.

I also attended a driving rally through some wooded and hilly countryside, where we were required to act as marshals at one of the check points. We arrived at the assembly point and after briefing were escorted to our check point locations. We were required to follow the leader who was driving an Austin Champ jeep.

Austin Champ jeep

This had independent suspension and was powered by a two litre Rolls Royce engine. He drove off a great speed along a rutted woodland path, and I tried to follow him in an old Willis jeep.

Willis jeep

The officer was hanging on for dear life as we hit tree root steps across the track, until after one large step he lost his hold and bounced right out of the jeep with a loud cry. Fortunately, he was not hurt and we had a good laugh about it. We did agree that if we went on a similar event we would make sure we used an Austin Champ.

Promotion

I was then sent on an Educational Instructors Course of three weeks' duration at the Royal Army Education Corps training centre at Celle. This was to enable me to run classes in the education centre. This was a hoot, of a course, with so much fun and humour mixed in with the learning.

The course content composed of the aspects of practical and technical skills training, as well as aspects of teaching academic subjects such as reading and writing.

The Director was a Lt Colonel in the RAEC, who on one occasion demonstrated his party piece, as an example of pure instructional technique. He appeared in his immaculate field service uniform complete with Sam Brown Belt, and proceeded to mix some plaster, which he used to plaster a wall, without spilling any and with not a spot on his uniform. He received a great round of applause.

On another occasion we were giving practice lessons to the group. One lad had the piece of chalk in his right hand and was sat on the corner of the desk. As he was talking to the class he was tossing the piece of chalk in his hand.

The director suddenly shouted, "99 change hands."

Which, whilst bringing the house down, was a good way to draw attention to the error in behaviour by the student.

While we were in Celle, we were taken to the site of the Bergen-Belsen Concentration Camp. What an experience that was. The atmosphere was very heavy, with no bird song, very silent and very ghost-like. The site was still being developed as a memorial to all those who were murdered in the camp, but had not reached the level of development that exists today. A very sober group of young men returned to Celle at the end of the visit.

Upon my return to my unit I was promoted to lance corporal, the stripe being required to supervise people whilst in the education centre. Being a lance corporal, I was entitled to use the corporals club, which was attached to the beer bar in the NAFFI. However, upon joining, there was an initiation process to go through. Behind the bar was a glass yard of ale, a long glass tube with a circular ball on the end. This was filled with ale at the new member's expense, who had to drink the contents at one go, some one and a half pints of beer. Of course the idea was to drink the beer in one go. If you had to stop and take a breath the beer splashed back up the tube and over your face. If this happened, the glass was refilled and the exercise repeated. The trick was not to remove the glass from your lips, as this allowed the air to enter the glass and agitate the beer, splashing it over the face of the drinker. I took three separate attempts before I was successful. Many organisations have a similar ceremony using a glass boot.

During the next nine months I paid two visits to 4 Base Workshops REME located in Bad Oeynhausen, to take firstly my second class draughtsman's badge and six months later my first class badge. In the workshops they had an operational drawing office, staffed by German civilians, where I worked for a week undergoing each test. It was just like being back at English Electric. Those badges were well worth having, as each one gave an increase in pay, called trade pay.

Opel Rekord

The next activity that I undertook was a brief secondment to 5 Infantry Workshops REME, were I worked on a project connected with that year's Monte Carlo Rally. A team of officers had persuaded Opel Motor Cars to lend them three Opel Rekord saloon cars, converted for rallying. They required a cardboard circle which fitted around the speedometer, to indicate the elapsed time. This required great accuracy in drawing the circles and the divisions all in Indian ink. The job took a week and was successful. And so it was back to Dortmund once more.

There was a lovely German cafe called Hous Hans, located in a typical German country cottage, run as a family concern. The food was superb and the beer excellent, serving Dortmunder Kronon, which was a lot better than the Dortmunder Union sold in the NAFFI. The speciality was a pork cutlet, the size of a dinner plate surrounded by beautiful chips. All our birthdays and other celebrations were held there. This was the only cafe in the area where no one tried any tricks like stealing glasses, ashtrays and beer. If you were caught, as some were, you were banned for life, and the proprietor meant it. On the occasion of my farewell meal when I was posted to 4 Base Workshops, the owner presented me with a set of his best pilsner glasses as a gift, which unfortunately did not last very long after I was demobbed.

Exercises

A great deal of our time was spent on exercises with other army units. There was always the threat that Russia might invade. Fortunately, she never did, but we had to be prepared. The largest exercise was a NATO one held in September, code named Battle Royal. We were based near Hanover for this exercise, with the HQ platoon located in a farm. The weather whilst we were there was awful, with very heavy rain. This reduced the farmyard to a sea of mud, with vehicles being continuously bogged down. This was the occasion when the QM couldn't find the supply depot and we existed on two small slices of corned beef and a spoonful of pom (dehydrated potato) three times a day for four days. On the third evening Johnny and I questioned why we were hungry when there was a large hen house full of laying hens. So at about 3am we entered the hen house and started collecting eggs, placing them in our battle dress blouses. Then we looked up and saw the farmer watching us. How he knew what we were doing, is still a mystery, as we had not made any noise. So, very sheepishly, we replaced the eggs and left.

Later in the morning the farmer came and asked us why we were stealing his eggs. We told him it was because we were very hungry. He then talked to his wife and gave us a couple of trays of eggs and a sack of potatoes. Boy, those eggs and chips were the best meal we had ever had. His wife then took us to a barn attached to the house which was where she had a large wooden tub which she used for her washing. This was filled with hot water and we were able to wash our clothes and ourselves, as two weeks in the same socks and underpants was not very hygienic.

When the time came to leave, we had to make the site spick and span. This involved removing the mud from the farm yard, which lowered the level by at least 10 inches. The farmer didn't bat an eyelid and we did wonder why.

Leave

Official wedding photograph

When we returned to barracks I found out that my request for UK leave had been granted and I travelled to England for three weeks leave, during which Jo and I were married on 16th October 1954 in St James Church, Chorley. I am proud to say that we are still together and celebrated our 62nd Wedding Anniversary this year. Our honeymoon was four nights in Morecambe, staying in a lovely bed and breakfast owned by an aunt of Jo's boss in the solicitor's office where she worked as a legal secretary.

Before I went home on leave to get married all the lads organised a big party for me in the NAFFI. In those days I had a part denture replacing two teeth in my top set. Well the long and short of it was that I had too much beer and upon going to bed had to sit up and with my head spinning, slowly slide down until I was lying down. This made my stomach revolt and I had to go to the toilet and be violently ill. It was confirmed the following morning that I had been wandering up and down the corridor naked, asking if anyone had found my denture. Of course not, it had gone down the toilet. Jo was not very pleased when I turned up for our wedding with two gaps in my teeth.

When I visited my grandparents, I presented them with a bottle of brandy. Granddad, having examined the bottle, commented on the poor quality of the brand. I asked him to taste a morsel, which he did and exclaimed that it was too good to drink on a daily basis, and that it should be saved for special occasions. I then explained what happened. A bottle of poor quality brandy was purchased and the contents emptied and replaced with best quality cognac. This could then be taken through customs as an opened bottle with no duty payable. The same procedure was used for cigarettes using opened packets. A totally different situation than which exists today.

I was met off the train at Dortmund Station by my pal Johnny who hung a notice around my neck saying BLIND MAN, and giving me a white stick to carry. The joke was working well until an MP spotted us and we had a few anxious moments of explanation. Fortunately, he saw the funny side of it and after removing the offending items we were allowed to go on our way.

Upon my return from leave, I was allowed to bring civilian clothing back with me. You were allowed to wear them when leaving barracks after six month's service. I brought back my Harris Tweed sports coat, brown contrasting slacks, pale blue shirt, tie and brown shoes, polished to army standards. I then had to parade in them before the OC, to ensure that they were up to standard. Mine were accepted and I wore them whenever I left the barracks for recreational purposes as listed on my licence.

When I arrived in Germany, some six years after the end of the war, things were getting back to normal, with many building sites and the building of factories and workshops. A good example was Coca Cola, who built a large bottling plant in Dortmund, which they were very proud of, to the extent that they organised trips to the plant for large groups of people. Our German Liaison officer was able to organise a visit for a 100 personnel from our unit. We travelled in two luxury coaches and enjoyed the tour of the plant and the visit to the staff canteen which followed it. Here we were introduced to a new drink of which the Coca Cola staff were very proud. It was with a great fanfare they introduced us to Rum & Coke. Well, you can imagine the joy with which we showed our hosts how we could drink this new drink. In every army unit there is often a young soldier who can sing a good song with a good voice and in a show-time manner. We had one, who on that evening took over the sound system and entertained us for a good hour. What a sing song it was. One hundred squaddies went home in the coaches with not a sober one amongst us, but with many thick heads the following morning.

The day before Ash Wednesday i.e. Shrove Tuesday, there was a carnival called the Mardi Gras. Johnny and I decided to go and watch the procession. We had to wear civvies, as uniforms were banned. Between us we could raise the return tram fares and the price of a couple of beers each. Having selected a suitable cafe with an upstairs balcony, we bought our first beer. A group of German people recognised us as soldiers and asked us to join them, which we did, and we didn't pay for another drink all night. Our new friends made sure that we caught the tram back to the Hauptfriedhop, the cemetery to us, and then we had to get back into camp as we were very late. This we achieved, with a small present for the duty sentry.

Nominated Driver

Dodge Ambulance

Life quickly resumed its normal pattern after my leave, with the addition that I was nominated as the driver of the unit bus. This vehicle was an American Dodge ambulance of wartime vintage which had been converted into a small people carrier for about 14 people.

My first trip was to take the unit rugby team to a game held on the airfield we used for driver training. Whilst the team was warming up one of our players sprained his ankle badly and couldn't play. Unfortunately, we had no reserves with us and I had to use the spare kit and take his place. I had never seen a game of rugby, never mind played in one. I was instructed to stay on the right wing and always pass the ball backwards. Shortly after the game started the ball came to me and I set of on a run for the line, when I hit something that felt like a brick wall. I don't remember much about the rest of the game after that. Upon inquiring who we had played I was told that it was only a team from the local Guards regiment, who were all over six-foot-tall and weighed at least 13 or 14 stones each. Never again. I always insisted that the reserves travelled after that.

On another famous occasion I drove the cricket team to Duisburg to play 4 Infantry Workshops. Here I found that I had to be an umpire. I was better qualified for this as I had played a lot of cricket as a youngster. The game started well, with us being the fielding side. Their opening batsmen were scoring well when there was an appeal for LBW. I leaned over to my right and stuck my figure in the air. The batsman gave me a filthy look and stalked back to the pavilion.

At the end of the innings we took tea, and the LBW batsman wearing his battle dress jacket with LT Col pips came to me and said, "That was never LBW corporal, but I always play the game, that was why I walked."

I was told on the way home that I had spoiled his figures as he normally scored at least a half century or more every week. We still lost.

Once I was driving the bus back to Dortmund in heavy rain grinding up a steep hill in Essen. The windscreen wipers on the Dodge vehicle were operated from the engine manifold using the vacuum to drive the wiper motor, which meant that when pulling hard in bottom gear up a hill, the wipers were moving very slowly, and when the top of the hill was reached, they sped up to their normal operating speed.

The traffic was heavy with lots of pedestrians on the pavements. I reached the top of the hill and changed gear, upon which the wiper blade whipped across the windscreen, became detached and flew like an arrow across the pavement and just missed an elderly gentleman. We didn't bother stopping to retrieve the blade, as he shook his fist at us.

Winter 1954

Christmas was a particularly difficult time of year. It was the first time I had not spent it with my parents and Jo. We had letters and Christmas cards to remind us of home and these did help somewhat. Still, the army tried their best for us. We had a large party in the NAFFI on Christmas Eve, when the amount of beer drunk must have been a record. Even the officers joined in, with the OC leaving to drive home and just managing to get past the barrier as the duty sentry struggled to open it. There were some very bad heads at breakfast on Christmas Day. Lunch on Christmas Day was the best meal I ever had in my two years. It was full of the usual Christmas fayre, with lots more beer and served by the Officers and Warrant Officers and Sergeants. A very good day, considering the circumstances.

In between Christmas and New Year's Eve, there was a celebration dinner in the Officers' Mess attended by all our officers including the OC. The following morning, I had just arrived in the Orderly Room when the telephone rang. It was the OC's wife enquiring after her husband. It transpired that he had gone to the dinner the previous evening, taking the car, but had not returned home. She thought that he had sensibly stayed the night, but she needed the car to go shopping and wanted a lift to the mess to collect the car. I agreed to collect her in the duty car to sort out her problem. When we arrived at the mess, the OC's car was there and she drove off using her spare set of keys. I then contacted our 3 IC to enquire were the OC was. When he had come round from a deep alcoholic sleep, and I told him the story, we went to the cloakroom and found the OC, still dead to the world, hanging from a hook with a coat hanger inside his uniform jacket. We sorted him out and both of us took him home, whereupon I was sworn to secrecy, and have kept my word until now. It was a very good laugh.

On New Year's Eve, Johnny and I agreed to baby sit for the CSM, as he and his wife were attending a dinner dance in the garrison mess. We duly arrived at his house to find the children in bed and asleep. As the CSM left the house he told us to help ourselves to the beer in the fridge. His wife whispered that we could cook a meal if we fancied one. So later in the evening after a couple of beers we raided the fridge and cooked the two lovely steaks for our supper and we returned to the barracks about 2.00 am in the morning. At lunch time there was a knock on the door to our room and upon opening it we found the CSM in full working dress, but in a foul mood. He then proceeded to call us all the names under the sun, after which he told us that the two lovely steaks we had eaten were for their lunch for today, and with an empty fridge he had to resort to a lunch in the mess, which required him to be properly dressed. We did have a good laugh, but only after he had gone.

A party of us were taken up in to the Harz Mountains for a winter exercise. The aim was to teach us how to work in winter weather. The fact that the lowest temperature read –

20°C and there was at least two feet of frozen snow, it could have been described as winter. It was so cold that a lorry could be driven over a frozen egg without breaking it. To crown it all we had to place our bottles of beer in a Dixie of hot water to defrost them before we could drink them. We slept in the wagons or anywhere where we were out of the wind. All we had in terms of extra kit was four blankets and a water proof sheet. We were taught how to make up a warm bed by laying a blanket on the ground and covering half of it with another one, until you had used all four blankets. You then folded the top halves over each other so that by lying inside the folds with four layers under your body and four layers on top, with the end folded under, you had a warm bed. To keep out the damp and cold, the water proof sheet was placed under and over the bed. The other requirement was to undress to your underwear and to sleep with your clothes next to your body with your boots under the top blanket. It sounds complicated but it did work. The CSM who was with us for the three nights we were on the exercise, took great delight in checking that we were following the rules, which according to him would prevent frost bite. None of use believed him and we were glad to return to barracks.

At this time, we had a Captain who was the 2 IC in the unit. He was not a very nice person, with many doubts about his parental background. He once held us on a Saturday morning muster parade in shirt sleeve order, until our arms were blue and people were starting to look decidedly under the weather. He only relented and dismissed the parade after the CSM had a very quiet word with him.

One morning whilst inspecting the living quarters, he opened my bedside locker without my permission or indeed without my presence. In the drawer he found an army pocket watch, which he confiscated and placed me on a charge for possessing stolen military property. In answer to the charge I informed him that the watch in question had been issued to my father during his career as a tank driving instructor with the RTR, during the war. I also pointed out the fact that the war office badge on the back had a surplus S stamped on it. The hearing was adjourned until my father could send the original receipt that he had received from the army when he paid for the watch upon demobilisation. A couple of weeks later I was marched into his office by the CSM, to be told that he had heard from my father and the matter was closed. I never did find out what my father said in his letter, but I did hear what the CSM whispered as we walked down the corridor.

A few weeks later that officer was posted away, and we had a very boozy party in the NAFFI to celebrate his leaving. This was followed by an announcement placed in Part 2 Orders requesting volunteers to join a Light Aid Detachment for deployment in Korea, only motor vehicle mechanics needed apply. Half of the motor mechanics platoon applied. When the lads were disembarking from the boat in Seoul, who should be waiting for them, but our old 2IC, who was their new LAD commander. Talk about jumping out of the frying pan into the fire, but we did hear that he eventually became a good officer who looked after his men.

One evening at the guard mounting, the orderly sergeant failed to turn up for duty. The following morning when arriving at the barracks he was placed on a charge and appeared before the OC to answer to the charge of, 'being absent without permission from a place of duty'. In reply to the charge he stated that his name did not appear on the day's orders. He informed the OC that as the officer had been awarded an MBE, the award was always added to his rank and name. He then informed the OC that as he, the orderly sergeant, had been awarded the BEM for service during the East Coast floods in 1951, that his full rank and name should include his BEM, and that this was missing from the day's orders. He therefore did not report for duty as his award was not included. The OC apologised for the apparent typing error and dismissed the charge. It would have been interesting to hear what the CSM said to the sergeant afterwards.

Spring 1955

2 ton trailer

We knew spring had arrived when we went out on exercises again. Coming back from our first one, I was driving an Austin 3 tonner with a 2-ton trailer on the hook when the clutch went. I had to wait until the recovery wagon came along. They hooked me up and we carried on. I had to sit in the body as the front wheels were off the ground and the steering was locked.

I was watching the trailer as we climbed up a steep hill, and wondered what would happen if the nut on the end of the tow bar came off, when it did! The trailer became detached, mounted the pavement and shot down a side street, hitting the front door of a house. Fortunately, it hadn't hit anyone. I screamed for the driver of the recovery vehicle to stop, which he did.

We recovered the trailer, re-assembled the tow bar, hitched it up again to my lorry and off we went. I often wondered what the owner of the house thought when he returned home to find a large hole punched in his front door.

One day the OC sent for me and gave me a task which he said I could do, as I was a mechanical engineering draughtsman. The task was to design and build a row of garage shelters to accommodate some unit vehicles during the winter.

The materials available were a large collection of scaffolding poles, clamps and sheets of corrugated iron. Where he had obtained these from it was better not to ask. I was given two general duty soldiers to help me.

The first task was to measure all the poles and sort them in to the different sizes, so that I knew what I had to work with. We also measured the various vehicles that would be sheltered, to ensure that the garages would fit them. So onto the drawing board, where I produced the working drawings required for the assembly.

Over the next two months the exercise was completed to everyone's satisfaction and I went on leave, where I spent two lovely weeks with my wife, in our first home together, mainly in bed.

235 Lyons Lane

This was a two up and two down terraced house owned by a local builder, who rented the house to us for £1 per week. Jo's dad had spent many hours decorating and modernising it for us, and we lived there for many years.

However, upon my return, I found that disaster had struck. One evening while I had been away, the whole edifice had blown over during a heavy gale. Fortunately, the vehicles were not under the shelter at the time. I was summarily ordered to sort out the problem. The whole structure was easily righted and then the problem was revealed. The lads who had assembled it had not inserted the ground spikes in the vertical pole base plates. When this error was corrected there was no further trouble. Was I glad that the whole problem was not my fault.

The sequel to the exercise was some four years later, when I was being interviewed for a design engineering position in the coal mining industry. When asked the question had I any experience in structural engineering I related the tale of the garages and was offered the position because of my honesty.

Summer 1955

In June we had to move the whole unit to the tank and artillery ranges for the annual range shoots. As an Infantry Workshops, we had to supply repair and maintenance services, so we were there for six weeks living under canvas. Thank goodness the weather was good, with no rain for the whole time we were there.

Johnny and I were in charge of the officers' mess, with an old Morris van used for cooking. We were actually based on the ranges at Celle and so the officers often dined in the mess at the garrison.

The morning after such an event I went into the OC's tent to tidy up. I entered the tent through the rear door, to be confronted by a pair of dress trousers, complete with his dress boots, bobbing up and down in the breeze. My first thought was that the OC had topped himself.

When I entered the tent from the front I saw that his trousers were fastened to a coat hanger by his braces, which was hooked on to the top of the wardrobe. What a relief.

Humber Estate

One evening I drove a party of officers to a dinner in the garrison mess, using the OC's Humber Estate Car. As we were driving back to camp a hare shot out in front of us and turned and ran down the road, clearly visible in the headlights.

The officer in the front passenger seat ordered me to catch up with the hare and as I drew close to it he opened the door which was hinged at the rear, so he could see the hare. When the front wheel was alongside it he told me to flick the wheel. This hit the hare and killed it.

We collected it and took it to the cookhouse where it was prepared and steeped in Claret to make a dish of Jugged Hare. Very good it was, as Johnny and I also had a share.

Matchless 500cc

It was on this exercise that I had my first and only trial ride on a motor cycle, a Matchless 500cc dispatch riders machine. I was given a five-minute course on the controls and sent on my way, wearing a dispatch riders helmet made of steel, which was very heavy. As I accelerated away by opening the throttle, a feeling of freedom and exhilaration came over me, followed by sheer panic when I looked at the speedometer and saw that I was doing over 65 mph. If I had fallen of the machine, I would have been badly scarred, as I was wearing only shorts and a tee shirt. I quickly decelerated, braked slowly, turned around and went back very carefully. Believe me I was very relieved to hand over the bike to its owner and swore that I would never ride one again.

The CSM organised a beer bar for the unit, so that we could socialise of an evening using the large marquee dining tent. The beer was bought from the NAFFI in the garrison, who charged a penny deposit on each bottle.

On the last night the CSM arranged to exchange the total bottle deposit fund for full bottles of beer, as the fund was in effect an illegal one. We had one of the best parties during my time in the unit.

Diamond T recovery vehicle

On the trip back I was to travel with the recovery section, in a Diamond T recovery vehicle, which was connected to a tank transporter trailer loaded with crates of spare parts. Our journey was timed to start at 4 am in order to miss the local traffic on the route to the autobahn. Everything was going well until we reached Hanover and we turned down a road to find that a building was covered in wooden scaffolding and was protruding into the roadway blocking our passage. We couldn't turn around or reverse back up the road. The recovery corporal who was driving took the decision to carry on, so we closed all the windows and drove down the road taking the scaffolding with us. Once we were clear we stopped and removed all the poles and planks of wood from the trailer and carried on our way, reaching Dortmund without any further problems.

Recreation

After a long exercise during which we had used many five-gallon jerry cans of petrol, diesel, and unleaded petrol for the cookers, all the dregs were collected into a couple of cans. We set off with them in the bus on a Saturday afternoon into the countryside to sell the mixture to a farmer for a few marks, to supplement our evening beer money. The other fiddle we were involved with was cigarettes. We could buy them for one shilling for twenty in the NAFFI, having been issued with cigarette coupons on pay parade. Our ration was 140 per week. In the orderly room we had an ex-English soldier who had married a German girl at the end of the war. He worked as our interpreter and therefore had the use of the German civilian canteen. He could sell our surplus cigarettes at the rate of one mark for twenty, a profit of 8.5 pence for us. This was invested in a travel fund which produced during my time two wonderful outings.

The first one was a day trip by coach along the valley of the River Rhine, taking in Düsseldorf and a superb lunch in a cafe near Koblenz. The day was ended with a party in a large night club in Cologne. It was here that it was decided that we needed a souvenir of the outing. On the wall was an illuminated toilet sign which looked rather valuable. One of the lads, an electrician, agreed to obtain it undercover of a sing song from the rest of us. This was duly acquired and we all departed on our way. How he did it without turning of the electricity we did not ask.

The second outing was a weekend visit to Brussels, with accommodation for the Saturday evening in an army barracks just outside the city. We had a very good time sightseeing and shopping for goods which you could not buy in England. In a shop full of Brussels lace I bought a box of lace handkerchiefs for my wife, paying in the local currency.

An elderly lady who was English, informed me in a whisper, "You can pay in Stirling."

In those days you could only take £30 pounds out of the country. I had to explain that we were English soldiers on an outing from Germany and did not have any Stirling.

The only other time that I had a problem with currency was when an aunt of mine used to bake a cake in an Oxo tin and place a £5 note under the cake and then send it to me in a parcel. You then had to find someone who was going home on leave, who would exchange the fiver for BAFSV (British Armed Forces Service Vouchers). The going rate of exchange was £4.50 in BAFVS.

Wednesday afternoons was always sports afternoon, when football and cricket games were organised. I always joined the swimming party. This was my sport when I was a pupil at Chorley Grammar School. The Dortmund swimming pool had been built for the 1936 Olympic Games and was not damaged during the war. The driver had to drive down a road which was designated as out of bounds to troops, as this was where the ladies of ill repute displayed their wares. The problem was it was the only way to get to the swimming pool, and so we broke the rules every week.

On Sunday afternoons we would go the Dortmund Football Stadium to watch the match, which we found was a totally different experience to watching two English teams play. I was then, obviously, a dedicated Preston North End fan, with Sir Tom Finney being my hero. The continental approach was very similar to the way the continental teams play today in the Champions League, with very little body contact and long developing attacks. This resulted in a very quiet crowd until the attacking team was in the penalty area, or when a goal was scored, when everyone went wild. The squaddies, a few thousand strong, however were cheering all the time in the English tradition.

Our favourite place when on exercises was a small village located near the Dutch border, where we used to set up camp on the local sports ground, much to the delight of the local children who loved to visit us and practice their English language skills. By this time my German was good enough for ordering food and drink or shopping for presents when going on leave. You can imagine my embarrassment when one day a little German girl, who was about eight or nine years of age, in very good English informed me that my German was that of a five-year-old pupil in her school. Deflation was very heavy in my mind.

This was the location where one young man nearly got himself in serious trouble with our OC, who had been out for the evening and returned to camp in the early hours of the morning. The young lad who was on guard duty challenged the OC, requesting from him the password of the day. The OC couldn't give it to him and so the young soldier called out the guard. I was guard commander that evening and recognising the OC allowed him to enter. The following morning it transpired that the Orderly officer, not knowing that the OC was leaving the camp had not given him the password. The young soldier was complemented on his correct approach to security.

One morning as we were waiting to use the thunder boxes, i.e. field toilets, there was another amusing incident. The procedure was, when occupying the box, you placed your belt over the canvas screen to signify that it was occupied. On this particular occasion a young lad came running up the hill to the site and finding that all the stalls were occupied began explaining in very strong language what he would do to the occupiers if they didn't hurry up.

As a belt was retrieved he commented, "About bloody time too."

You can imagine the look on his face when the OC pulled aside the screen and with a stony face marched away. We all collapsed with laughter, and the young soldier spent all day worrying if he would be put on a charge.

In the summer the Quarter Master Sergeant was promoted and posted and he arranged a very lavish farewell event for him and his wife in the Sergeants' Mess. This was to be a supper dance with everyone in dress uniforms, with their wives in beautiful gowns. Johnny and I agreed to act as waiters, at a price of course, because it was on a Saturday evening. To keep up with the theme, we were wearing dress uniform trousers, white shirts and black bow ties. Didn't we look smart! Part of the deal was to supervise the cooking of a large pot of curry made from compo rations. Just before serving, the QMS came into the kitchen and tasted the food, which he found was a bit bland, so he added a full tin of curry powder to hot it up and increase the beer sales after supper.

At about 1.30am Johnny and I were cleaning up when the door opened and in came the WO1. He apparently had lost the top set of his dentures and enquired if we had found them. We searched among the streamers and decorations which were littering the floor and low and behold we did find them. We often wondered how he came to lose them on the dance floor.

Autumn 1955

September 1955 came around again, and it was time for the NATO exercise Battle Royal once again. As in the previous year we returned to the location in the farm yard. Lo and behold what did we find? A new concrete farm yard, complete with a drainage system, walls and gate, paid for by the UK government. There were some other improvements that year as well, as the QM did not lose the supply depot, so the food was better. The highlight of the event was when I drove the OC to the local American Army unit for lunch one day. He ate with the officers and I ate with the soldiers. What a spread of food! It was even better than what we had in barracks. I even had ice cream - what a luxury. We also experienced the indulgence of a visit to a mobile laundry and bath unit, which meant clean clothes and bodies after nearly two weeks without a change. We'd tried to keep our feet clean by wearing sea boot stockings, with gum boots and liberal coverings of army issue foot powder, which was marvellous stuff. One evening we were entertained by the sight of two tanks being loaded on their tank transporter trailers by the drivers from the Royal Tank Regiment, which was my dad's regiment during the war.

Two days before the end of the exercise, I received the biggest shock of my time as a national service soldier. It was published on Part Two Orders that I had been promoted to the rank of acting sergeant and posted to 4 Base Workshops, at Bad Oeynhausen with effect from 1st October. This was four days after our return to barracks. This did not leave much time for organising my departure, including a farewell meal at Hous Hans for my friends. So on the morning of my departure, feeling very apprehensive, I went for breakfast wearing my best uniform with the three stripes on my arm.

6 Infantry Workshops stayed in Dortmund until 1957 when it moved to Hamm. The barracks were occupied by various units until 1976, when it was occupied by the Cornwall Girls Boarding School until 1993, when the school was closed.

4 Base Workshops

Bad Oeynhausen station today

I travelled from Dortmund to Bad Oeynhausen by train and arrived at the workshops as the civilian workers were leaving. There were so many of them, it reminded me of finishing work at English Electric.

I was introduced to the person that I was to share a room with, who filled me in on how the unit worked. His name was Peter, a qualified carpenter who worked in the workshop which restored all wood work on the vehicles. We became very good friends.

Willis jeep   14 ton Leyland lorry

Volkswagen Beetle,   Austin 3 ton lorry,

The workshops were based in the ex-Eisenwerk Weserhutte factory, which made earth removing equipment before and during the war, very similar to JCB in England. The workshops were used to completely refurbish a wide range of army vehicles including Jeeps, Scamell Recovery Tractors, Austin and Bedford 3 ton lorries and 14 ton Leyland lorries, and strangely, a line for Volkswagen Beatle cars

Scammell recovery tractor   Bedford 3 ton lorry

Every workshop was staffed by German civilian workers, on modern flow line procedures, with a member of army personnel acting as the liaison supervisor of the particular trade in that workshop. My role was liaison in the drawing office, due to my having my Al Mechanical Draughtsman Trade badge. Of course I was well acquainted with this arrangement because it was where I had taken both my trade tests. Thus I settled into the last four months of my service. Which were anything but boring as I will describe.

My duties in the drawing office included getting the 10 draughtsmen to accept me as an asset to the working of the office. This could have been difficult as they had a German Civilian Chief Draughtsman who supervised and checked their work. I achieved this by taking the next job which came in. This was a gearbox from an Austin 3 Tonner. The job was to measure the casing and produce a working drawing for the foundry to produce several copies, and for the castings to be machined ready for assembly. This I did without any great difficulty and the drawings were checked by the Chief Draughtsman to his satisfaction, and so I was accepted as someone who knew what he was about.

A very strong line of gossip was about a member of staff who had a VW Beetle, which required refurbishing. He changed the colour to army green, obtained a set of false documents and left it in the storage area. It was duly placed in the programme and upon completion he collected it and had it resprayed to its original colour. A brand new car, at no cost to him.

Life was good at 4 Base Workshops, no parades, no bulling of kit etc., although we were trusted to always be very smart and tidy in our dress. The pace of life was very pleasant, unless you were on duty as security officer. This meant being on the gate when the workers were arriving for work at 7.00am and checking their passes. You were also required to be at the gate when they were leaving at 5.30pm. The biggest problem was the stealing of material and spare parts for sale on the local black market. The solution was to search a random selection of people, searching bags and giving a rub down. If we were feeling in a difficult mood, or there was a suspicion of enhanced thieving, we would search everybody. This meant that the last person left the factory at 7.30pm. The result was a decrease in thieving for quite some time thereafter.

One of the duties that I was given as the latest and junior member of staff, was to sleep in an empty quarter overnight to prevent civilians occupying the premises as squatters. This was a very boring duty until one evening I was recalled to the base late at night. Walking back, I came to the main crossroads of the town which had railings around the corners. These were to make people walk around the corner and use the pedestrian crossing. Well, being it was late at night, with no traffic, I jumped over the railings to cross the junction.

Whereupon a German policeman stepped out of a doorway and in good English, said, "Good evening Sergeant Burkey, would you please jump over the railings and go back to the other side of the road and then cross the correct way?"

I did this feeling a right idiot. This was a good example of the high standards of German pedestrian road safety that I believe is still in use today, according to a friend who went to Germany on holiday recently.

Nearly Over

As a sergeant I was entitled to 10 days' local leave, which could be spent in the UK provided that I paid my own return fares. This I agreed to do, but before describing this event, another one of great importance took place. This was the garrison Christmas party and dance, which every member of staff was required to attend. So Peter and I duly turned up looking very smart in our best uniforms.

The evening was a great success, apart from one slight problem. There was a member of staff who point blank refused to dance and had done so all his life. So his attractive wife latched on to Peter and I and informed us that she was not going to miss any dance and that we would assist her in achieving her target, by dancing with her and no other lady. By the end of the evening both of us were completely exhausted, but happy that we had achieved the set target.

Shortly after this event I went home on leave, after having to solve yet another problem. I had received a letter from my wife informing me that she had obtained two tickets for the Young Conservatives Christmas Eve Dinner Dance. This was a black tie event, being the premier event in the town's calendar. My wife had bought herself a beautiful dress, but I did not own a dinner jacket. So Peter and I put our heads together and came up with an acceptable solution. This was that I would wear his number one blue dress uniform, which with a small alteration would fit me, and was an acceptable substitute for a dinner jacket.

Dress blues

The evening was a great success with excellent food and good music. Jo and I left at 11.15pm so that we could attend Midnight Communion at St James Church. My appearance in dress blues caused some comments from my friends, who thought that I had become a regular soldier, as national servicemen were not issued with dress blues. That Christmas was totally different from the previous one, which Jo and I spent together doing all the things we did at normal Christmases, particularly lunch with my mum and dad and tea two hours later with Jo's mum and dad.

In the New Year at the end of my leave, I returned to Germany to complete my service being due for demobilisation on 3rd February 1956. First of all, I had to attend the monthly unit dance, where I was duly presented with an engraved tankard. This was, as per the tradition, filled with a shot from each optic from behind the bar, for me to drink in one go. Wow, what a kick! Thankfully someone was standing behind me in case it knocked me over.

I finally departed for England on 20th January which was a lovely birthday present. The train journey to the Hook of Holland was quite uneventful until the train reached Krefeld. A sergeant from the Royal Army Education Corps joined us in the sergeant's coach wearing a guard's headdress. As the train passed their camp he threw the hat out of the window and it just skimmed over the fence.

"That will cause them a problem," he said as he pulled his RAEC blue beret from his case, informing us that he'd had to suffer purgatory for 18 months having to wear the dreaded hat. So we settled down to a good meal and wine to help us on our way.

When we arrived at the dock, there were no officers travelling so we were allocated to the officer's quarters, complete with bunk beds and clean sheets and pillow cases. Having collected a goodly supply of beer we all had a very happy crossing.

On the journey from Harwich to Manchester on the North Country Boat Train, I was joined in my compartment by a member of the RAF, complete with his wife, two children, push chairs and suitcases. Having helped them to settle in, he opened one of his cases and produced a bottle of whiskey, which we shared.

When the train arrived in Manchester as I walked along the platform I could see Jo waiting for me at the barrier. The problem was I could see two of her, but fortunately I did kiss the correct one. Thus, ended my National Service.

Civvy Street

When we arrived home and we had had a meal, Jo informed me that St James CLB were having their prize-giving evening and asked if I wanted to go. What an offer, of course I did, so out came the uniform, which in those days was blue serge and stand up collar, with brass buttons. It was pressed, the buttons polished, the leather and brass belt bulled and off we went. It was wonderful to meet so many of my friends and to be welcomed back to the organisation that I truly loved.

On the Sunday morning we went to church and it was very emotional to see Jo singing in the choir wearing her blue robe. After lunch, I picked up the Sunday Paper and settled down for a lazy afternoon.

"Oh no," said Jo. "You are coming with me."

So under some duress I went with her to the church Sunday school where I was introduced to my class. My wife and the superintendent had arranged this without telling me. I did wonder if my RAEC Instructors Certificate would help, which fortunately it did: and so began my involvement with the school which lasted for many years.

I then went to the personnel department at English Electric Company to hand over my discharge papers and to claim my job back. So on 1st February I was back in the drawing office. It was lovely to see that the whole team were still there and I went back on the same drawing board that I had left two years ago. How time flies when you are having fun!

The final tie with my national service came in the July, when Jo and I went on holiday with my mum and dad to the Isle of Wight. As we had travelled in dad's car we were able to meet Johnny in Folkestone on our way home. In November my eldest daughter was born which was the start of our family life.

At the time of the Suez Canal episode I was sweating as to whether or not I would be recalled, as was one of my friends, who spent 3 weeks unloading and loading ships in Port Said harbour, before returning home and being demobbed for the second time.

A friend who lived in Chorley and was in Germany at the same time as me, was retained in service for a further six months; and therefore served for two and a half years.

I finally said goodbye to the army when I received a letter from REME records, requesting me to send my army uniforms and kit to RAOC Donnington, using a railway warrant. The porter at the station did not want to accept it, so in a flash of bloody mindedness I dumped the whole lot on his counter and walked out, feeling great.

Veterans Badge and National Service Medal

National service soldiers as a group were not treated very well by the government of the day. Some were killed in action, others wounded and very many just wasted two years of their lives, with no reward or acknowledgement. The only award, apart from any campaign medals, a national service soldier can legally wear, is the Veterans Badge and the National Service Medal issued by the Royal British Legion, both of which have to be paid for.

So what had I obtained from my two years? I had learned to drink large quantities of beer, although upon returning home I didn't have any for the next six months. I had developed both mentally and physically with a great deal of self-confidence, and had achieved more qualifications and a higher rank then most people did normally. Therefore, the answer was, in my case, a worthwhile experience, as I went in as a boy and came out as a man and all at the Government's expense.

ABOUT THE AUTHOR

William Burkey served an engineering apprenticeship with The English Electric Company in Preston, before national service with the Royal Electrical & Mechanical Engineers. He then worked as a design engineer in the aircraft and mining industries and lecturer in Engineering. In 1970 he was appointed to the post of Deputy Chief Education Officer in The Home Office, Prison Department, with responsibility for Vocational Training Courses for inmates of Prisons and Borstals. Following Prison Education re-organisation in 1988 he spent the rest of his working life in personnel, computer training and teaching a wide range of subjects in a range of schools. He is currently living in retirement on the Costa del Sol in Spain with his wife of many years, near his daughter, the novelist Wendy Cartmell, who inspired this book.

Boyhood Blitz

Boyhood Blitz is one boy's account of the struggles of an ordinary British family before, during and after World War II. The book is a fascinating depiction of his life during the Blitz in Wallasey, evacuation to the countryside and eventual relocation to Lancashire. This upbeat, adventurous account, is a must read for adults and children alike. Social history at its best!

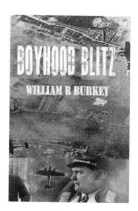

Now available from your local Amazon store.